Writing

This book belongs to

....

Place your star sticker here
when you complete a page.
See how far you've come!

Author: Carole Asquith

How to use this book

- Find a quiet, comfortable place to work, away from distractions.

- This book has been written in a logical order, so start at the first page and work your way through.

- Help with reading the instructions where necessary and ensure that your child understands what to do.

- This book is a gentle introduction to writing. By working through the activities, your child will begin to put pencil to paper and develop on to letter formation. Encourage your child to develop a tripod grip when showing them how to hold a pencil. The use of the right or left hand is fine at this stage; it is normal for young children to use both hands before showing a preference.

- If an activity is too difficult for your child then do more of our suggested practical activities (see Activity note) and return to the page when you know that they're likely to achieve it.

- Always end each activity before your child gets tired so that they will be eager to return next time.

- Help and encourage your child to check their own work as they complete each activity.

- Let your child return to their favourite pages once they have been completed. Talk about the activities they enjoyed and what they have learnt.

Special features of this book:

- **Stickers:** to be used in activities where instructed. The stickers are labelled with the page number, indicating where they are to be placed.

- **Progress chart:** when your child has completed a page, ask them to stick the relevant star on the first page of the book. This will enable you to keep track of progress through the activities and help to motivate your child.

- **Activity note:** situated at the bottom of every left-hand page, this suggests further activities and encourages discussion about what your child has learnt.

- **Certificate:** the certificate on page 24 should be used to reward your child for their effort and achievement. Remember to give lots of praise and encouragement, regardless of how they do.

Published by Collins
An imprint of HarperCollins*Publishers* Ltd
1 London Bridge Street
London SE1 9GF

HarperCollins*Publishers*
Macken House, 39/40 Mayor Street Upper,
Dublin 1, D01 C9W8, Ireland

© HarperCollins*Publishers* Ltd 2026

10 9 8 7 6 5 4 3 2 1

ISBN 978-0-00-877531-5

First published 2026

A Catalogue record for this publication is available from the British Library.

Author: Carole Asquith
Publisher: Fiona McGlade
Project editor: Chantal Addy
Design and layout: Ian Wrigley
Cover design: Sarah Duxbury and Amparo Barrera
All images © Shutterstock.com and © HarperCollins*Publishers*
Production: Bethany Brohm
Printed in India by Multivista Global Pvt. Ltd.

MIX
Paper | Supporting responsible forestry
FSC
www.fsc.org
FSC™ C007454

Contents

Straight lines

● These tractors are making their way to the barn after working in the field. Use a pencil to show them the way along the dotted lines. Place the missing barn stickers to complete the activity.

Use pincer tongs or easy grasp plastic tweezers to move small objects such as beads from one bowl to another to encourage pincer development.

Place the missing stickers of the skiers, then use a pencil to join the dots to help them ski to the finish line.

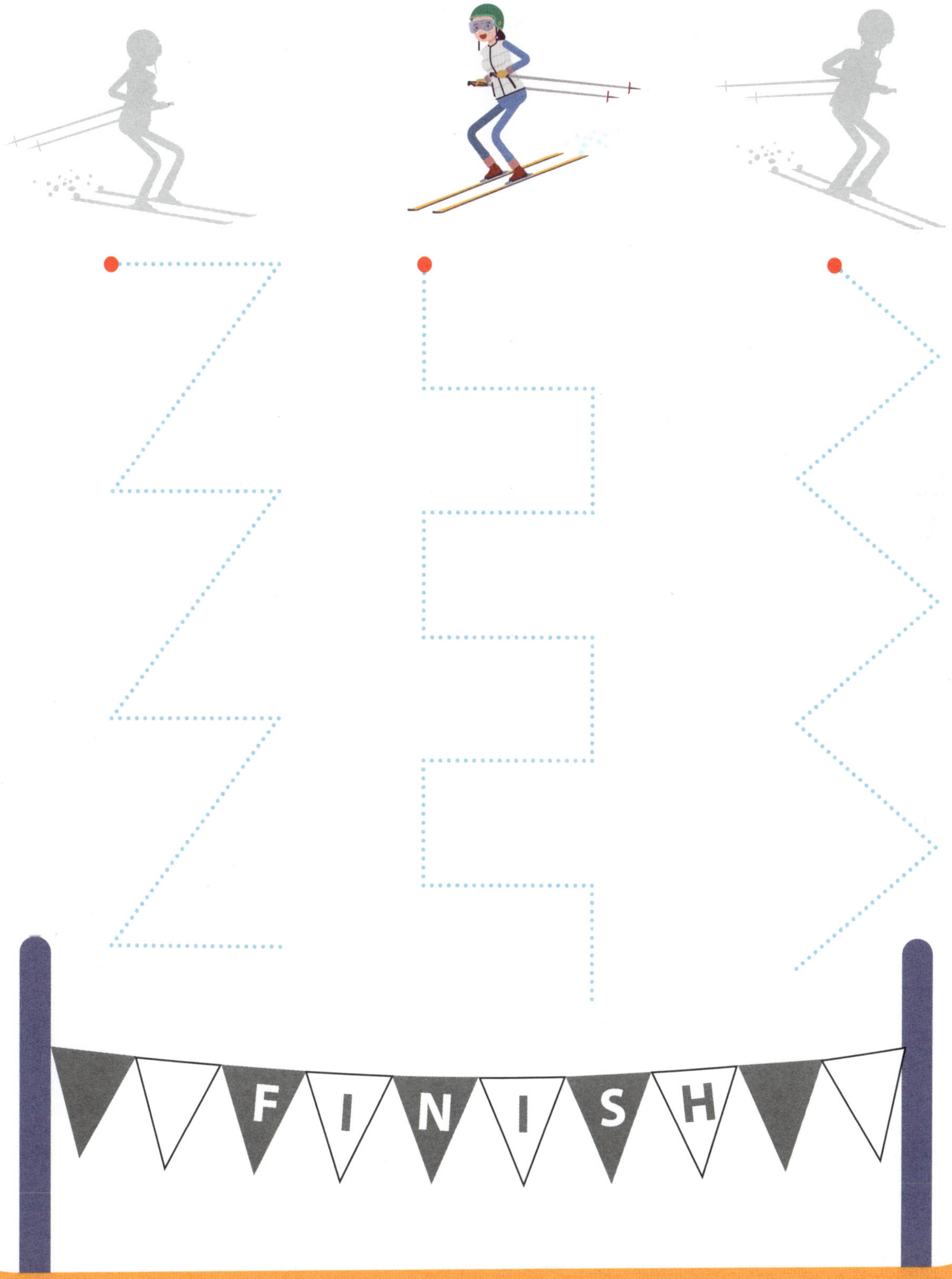

FINISH

Curvy lines

● Start on the dots and use your pencil to help the bees find their way to the hives. Place the missing hive stickers to complete the activity.

These little birds are flying home to their nests. Join the dots to show them the way, then place the missing nest stickers to complete the activity.

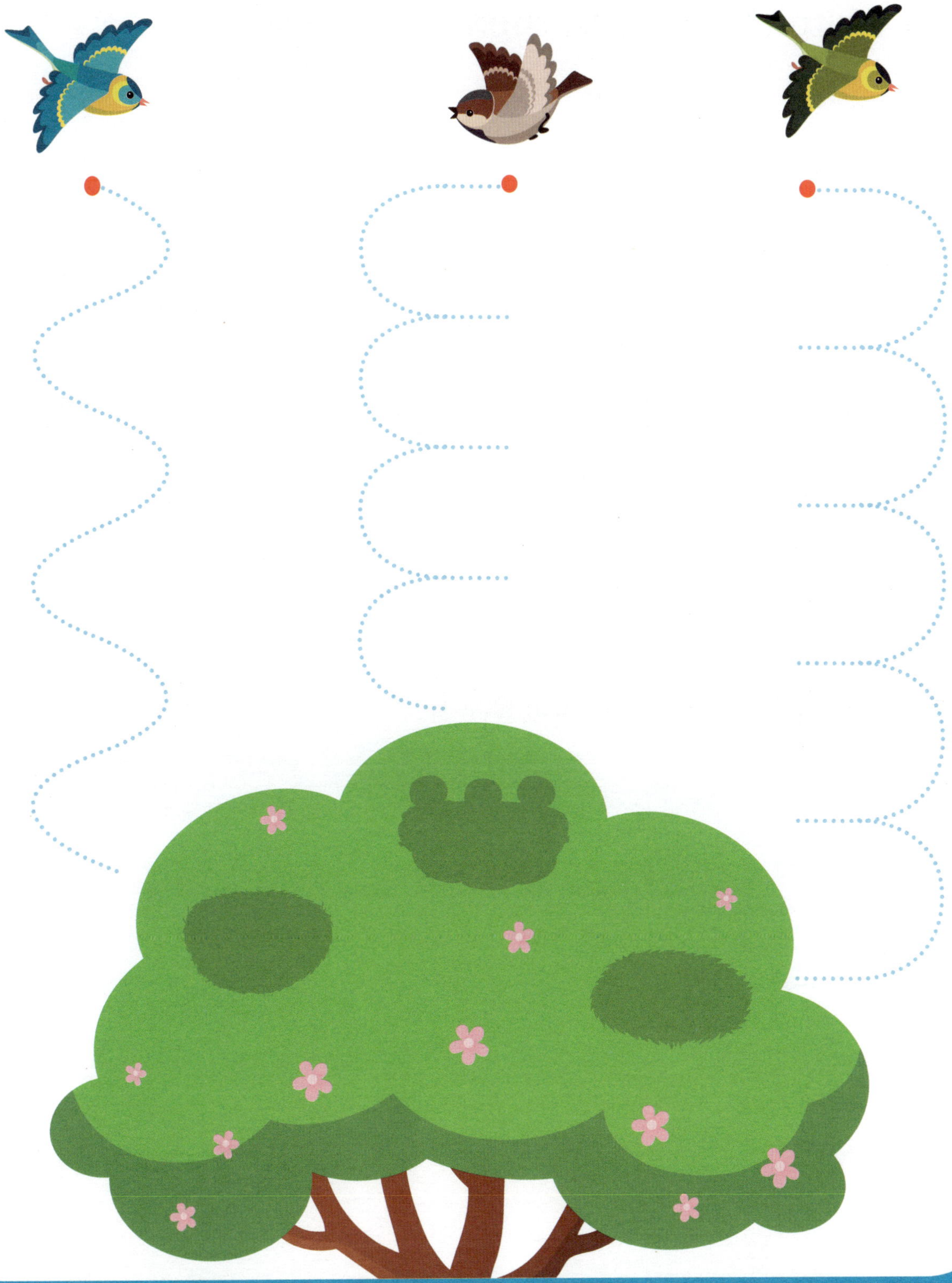

Well done! Add your star stickers to page 1.

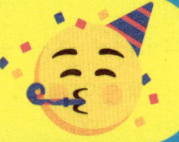

Letters c, o, a and d

- Trace the letters with your finger. Using your pencil, start on the red dot and follow the arrows to write the letters, then try by yourself.

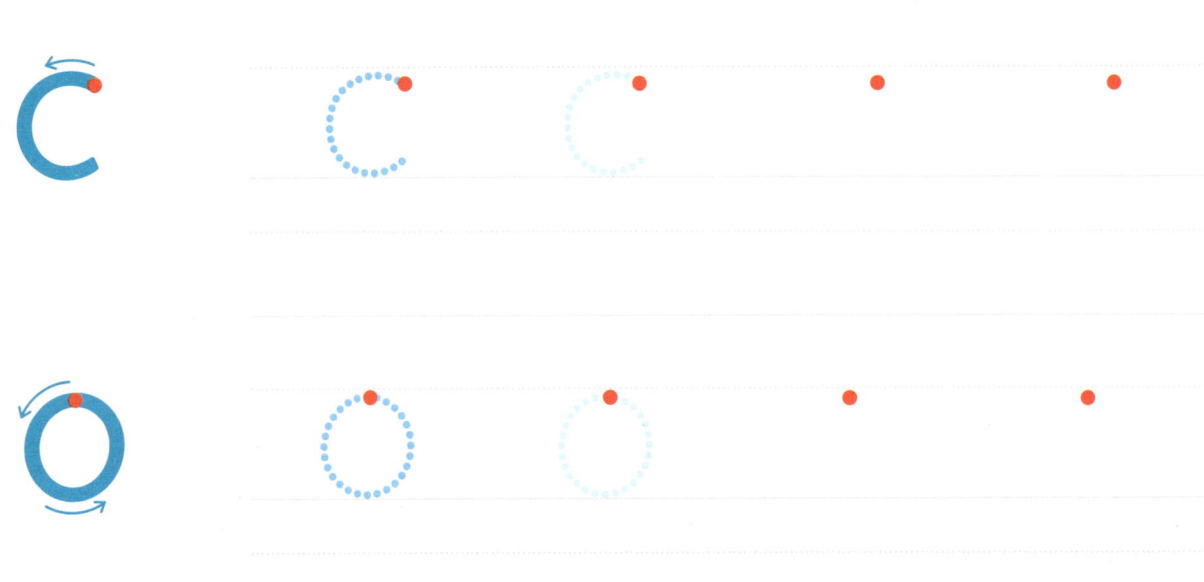

- Place your octopus and crab stickers to complete the underwater picture.

crab

octopus

- Trace the letters, then try writing them by yourself. Place your picture stickers for each letter.

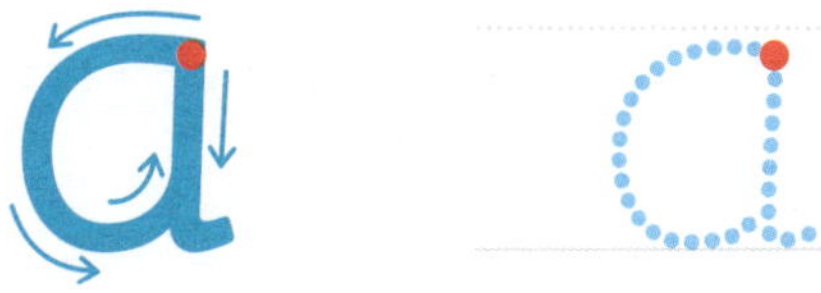

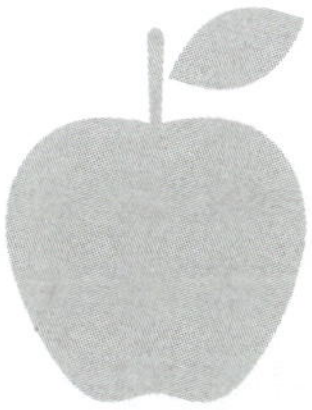

a   a   a   •   •

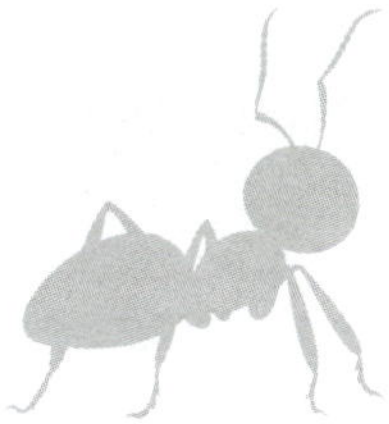

apple

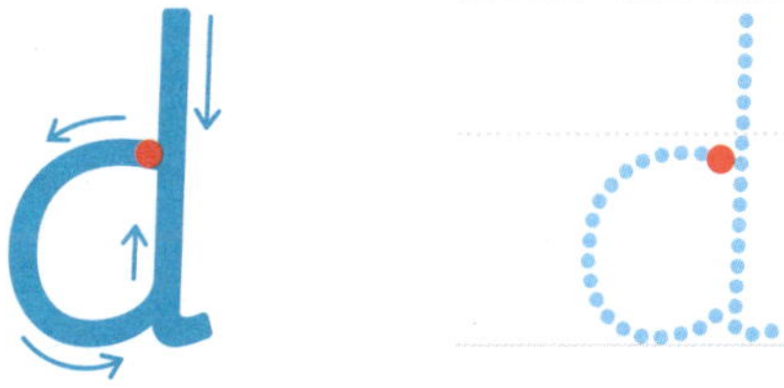

ant

d   d   d   •   •

duck

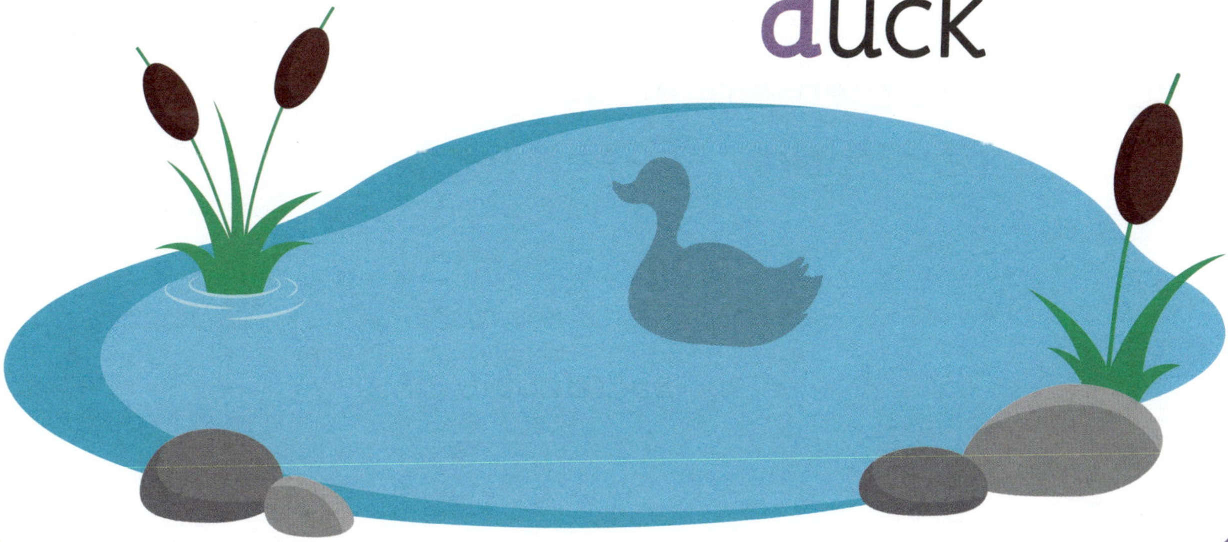

Letters g, q, e and s

- Trace the letter **g** quickly so the Billy Goats Gruff can cross the bridge before the troll catches them! Try writing the letter by yourself, then place your picture sticker.

goat

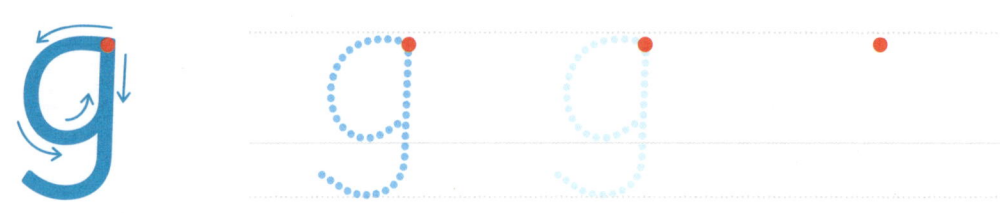

- Trace the letter **q**. Try writing the letter by yourself, then place your picture sticker.

queen

q

Wipe-clean boards and marker pens are a great way to encourage your child to practise letter shapes as they can easily be erased. This helps them to write with more independence and confidence.

● Trace the letters, then try writing them by yourself. Place your stickers to find the animals in the jungle.

e   e   e   e   ·   ·

s   s   s   ·   ·

snake

elephant

Well done! Add your star stickers to page 1.

11

Letters i, r, l, t and k

● Trace the letters, then try writing them by yourself. Place your picture stickers for each letter.

i

insect

ink

r

rocket

Practise air-writing on your child's back. See if they can guess which letter you have drawn then ask them to write one on your back. It's great fun guessing the letters!

12

5   7   9   11   13
4   6   8   10   12
15   17   19   21   23
14   16   18   20   22

Page 4

Page 5

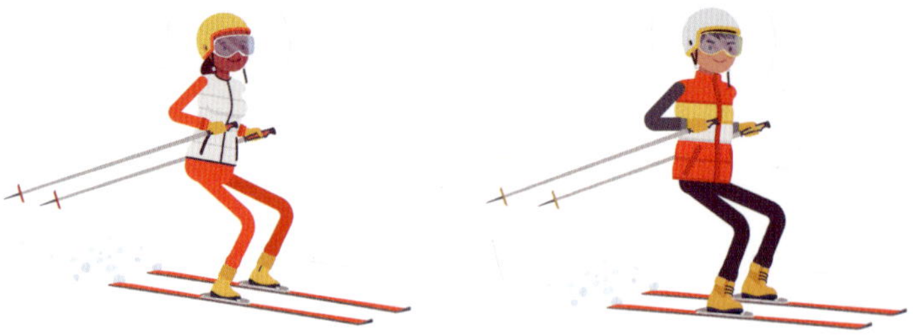

Page 6

Page 7

Page 8

Page 9

Page 10

Page 11

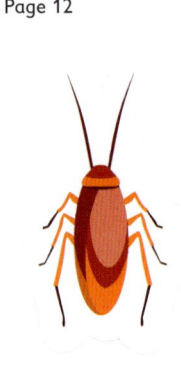

Page 12

Page 13

Page 14

Page 15

Page 16

Page 17

Page 18

Page 19

Page 20

Page 21

Page 22

Page 23

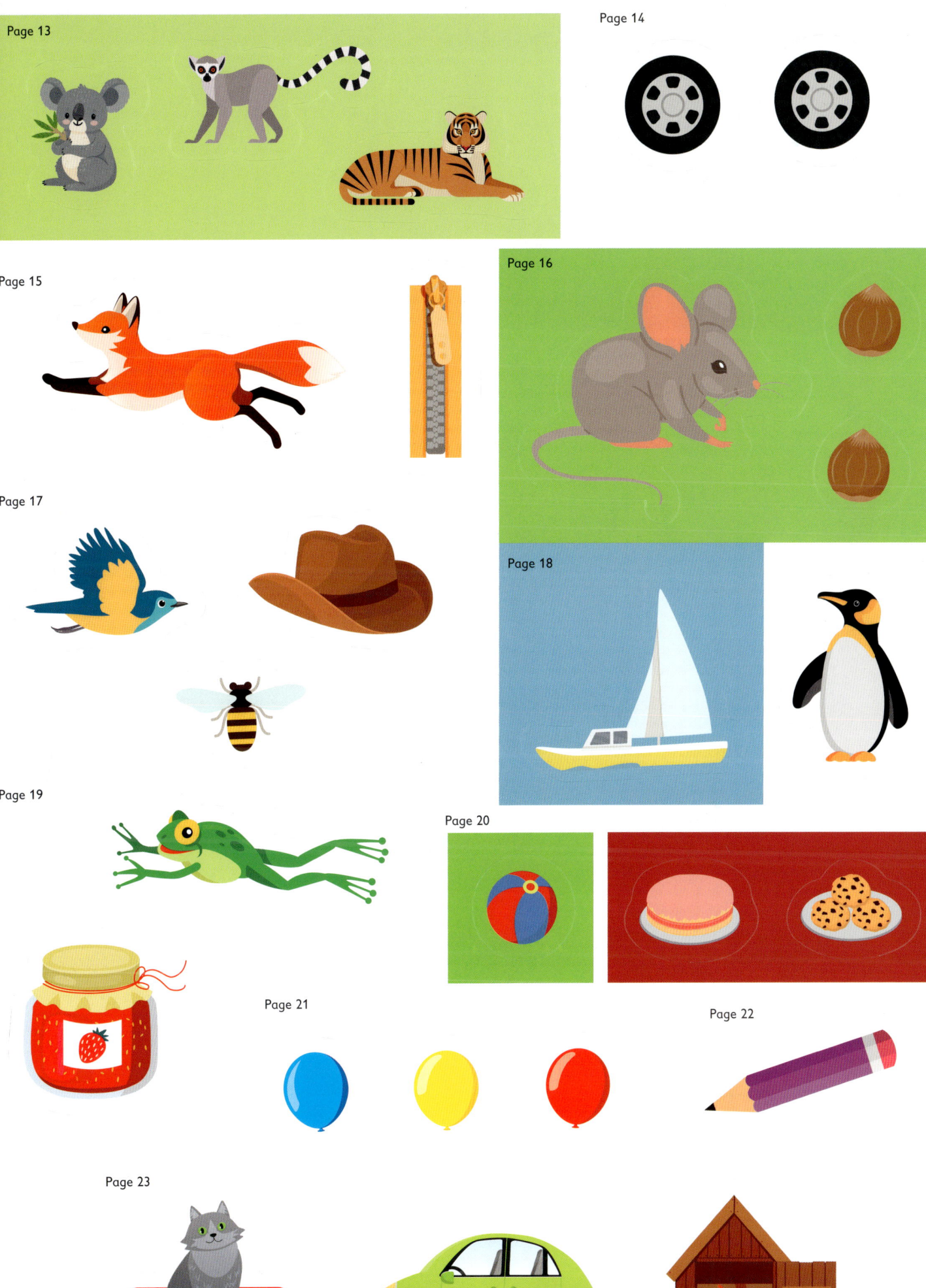

l l l l l

t t t t t

k k k k

lemur

koala

tiger

train

Well done! Add your star stickers to page 1.

Letters v, w, z and x

- Trace the letters, then try writing them by yourself.

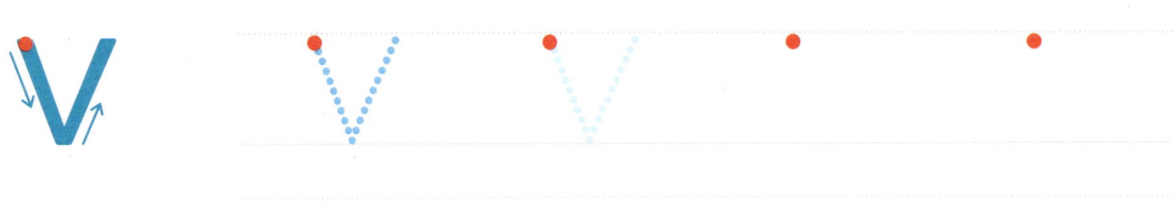

- Place your wheel stickers on the van.

van

wheel

- Trace the letters, then try writing them by yourself. Place your picture stickers for each letter.

Z z z

zebra

zip

X x x

fox

box

Well done! Add your star stickers to page 1.

15

Letters n, m, h and b

- Trace the letters, then try writing them by yourself.

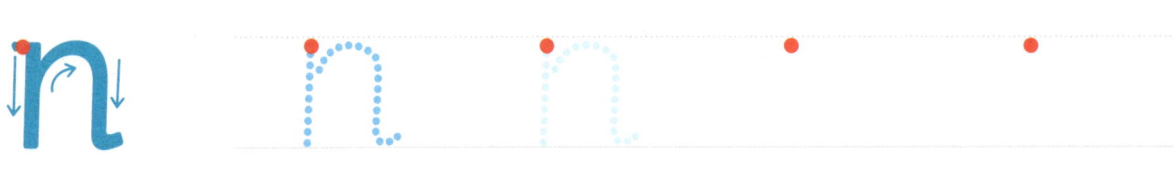

- Use your stickers to help the mouse find the nuts.

mouse

nut

Use counters or beads to make the shapes of letters using the correct orientations to help with letter formation skills. It's great for developing fine motor skills too!

Trace the letters, then try writing them by yourself. Place your picture stickers for each letter.

h   h   h

hippo

hat

b   b   b

bee

bird

Well done! Add your star stickers to page 1.

17

Letters p, y, j and f

● Trace the letters, then try writing them by yourself. Place your picture stickers for each letter.

p p p

penguin

pear

y y y

yacht

Use large sheets of paper and write letters on them. Let your child drive toy cars or trace them with a paint brush. Make it fun and always give lots of encouragement and praise as they develop these early skills.

j

jam

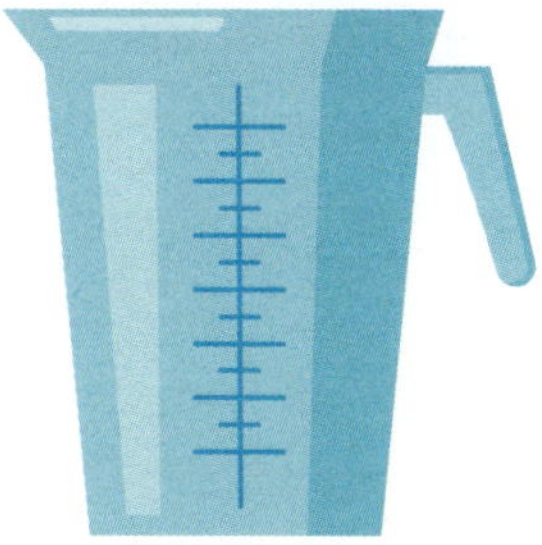

jug

f

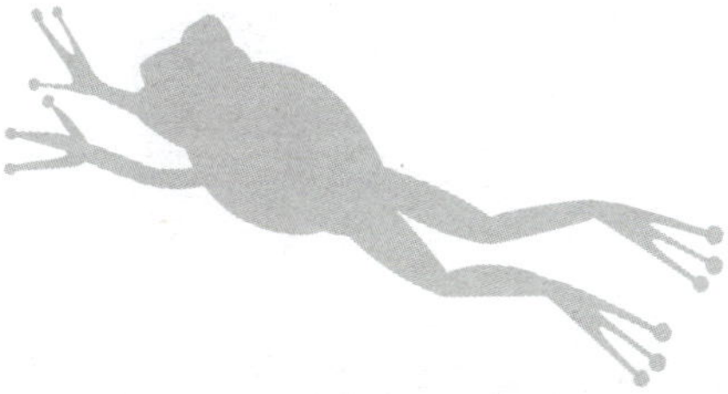

frog

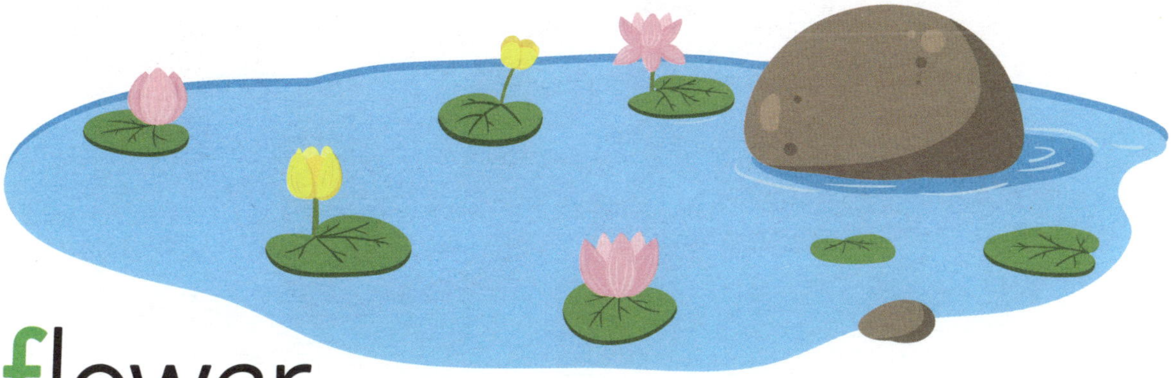

flower

Well done! Add your star stickers to page 1.

Writing words

- Now you have practised all your letters, you can try writing words. Trace over all the letters in the words.

can   see   I   dad

mum   like   my

- Place your stickers to complete the picture.

Randomly select magnetic letters from a basket and ask your child to copy the letter shapes using the correct formation.

Making sentences

Trace over the letters in each sentence, then place your stickers to complete the picture below.

I can see my mum.

I can see my dad.

I like my mum.

I like my dad.

Well done! Add your star stickers to page 1.

21

Let's write your name!

- Ask a grown-up to write the letters of your name on the line for you to trace.

- Now try writing your name by yourself.

- Place your sticker to complete the picture.

Try setting up a role-play area using a selection of writing and drawing equipment. A café for them to pretend to write menus or food orders is a great way to encourage early writing skills.

Writing a sentence

● Trace over the words in these sentences, then place your stickers to complete the pictures.

Dad has a green car.

The cat is on the mat.

The hen is in the hut.

Well done! Add your star stickers to page 1.

23

Certificate
of
Achievement

Well done!

This certificate is awarded to

....

for successfully completing

....

Age ....   Date ....

Signed ....